FEELINGS

1

Anger

Tamra B. Orr

Published in the United States of America
by Cherry Lake Publishing
Ann Arbor, Michigan
www.cherrylakepublishing.com

Reading Adviser: Marla Conn MS, Ed., Literacy specialist, Read-Ability, Inc.

Photo Credits: © Andrey Arkusha/Shutterstock Images, cover, 1; © ladybirdstudio/Shutterstock Images, 4; © tusharkoley/Shutterstock Images, 6; © nathapol HPS/Shutterstock Images, 8; © Daniel Jedzura/Shutterstock Images, 10; © pixelheadphoto/Shutterstock Images, 12; © cherylcasey/Shutterstock Images, 14; © wckiw/Shutterstock Images, 16; © laolaopui/Shutterstock Images, 18; © Blend Images/Shutterstock Images, 20

Library of Congress Cataloging-in-Publication Data
Names: Orr, Tamra, author.
 Title: Anger / Tamra B. Orr.
Description: Ann Arbor : Cherry Lake Publishing, 2016. | Series: Feelings | Audience: K to Grade 3. | Includes bibliographical references and index.
Identifiers: LCCN 2015048092| ISBN 9781634710411 (hardcover) | ISBN 9781634711401 (pdf) | ISBN 9781634712392 (pbk.) | ISBN 9781634713382 (ebook)
Subjects: LCSH: Anger—Juvenile literature.
Classification: LCC BF575.A5 O77 2016 | DDC 152.4/7—dc23
LC record available at http://lccn.loc.gov/2015048092

Cherry Lake Publishing would like to acknowledge the work of The Partnership for 21st Century Learning. Please visit www.p21.org for more information.

Printed in the United States of America
Corporate Graphics

Table of Contents

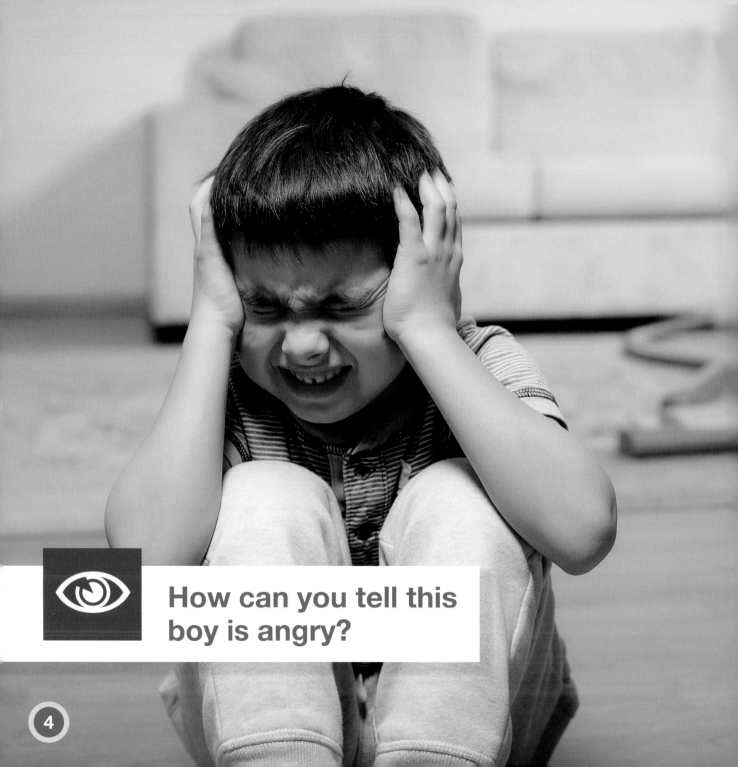

How can you tell this boy is angry?

When I'm Angry

Sometimes I get angry.

The anger starts inside. My face feels hot. It gets red.

When the anger comes out, I yell.
I **stamp** my feet.

Why I'm Angry

Mom says I get angry when I'm tired.

Dad says I get angry when I'm hungry.

Usually I need a hug, a nap, or a **snack**.

Why do you think these friends are fighting?

Who Makes Me Angry

Sometimes my friends make me angry.

They don't share their toys.

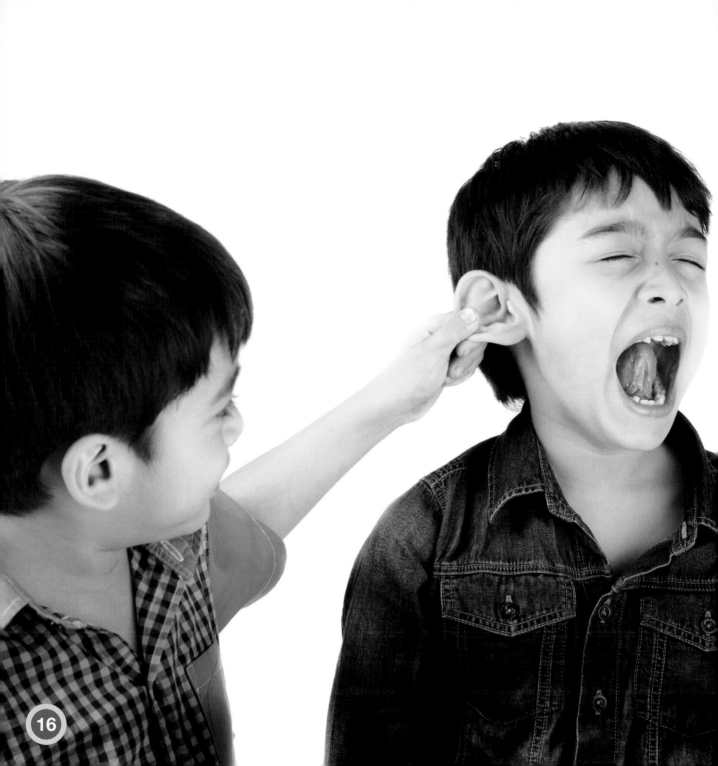

I get mad at my brothers, too.

They **tease** me. It's not funny!

Letting Go of Anger

Everyone gets angry sometimes.

It's not fun to be angry, though.

I take a deep **breath** and wait.

Soon, my anger is all gone.
I'm glad!

Find Out More

Adler, Esther. *Angry: Helping Children Cope with Anger*.
New York: Bright Awareness Publications, 2014.

Lite, Lori. *Angry Octopus: An Anger Management Story*. Marietta,
GA: Stress Free Kids, 2011.

Glossary

breath (BRETH) the air a person brings in and sends out of their lungs
snack (SNAK) a small bit of food to eat
stamp (STAMP) to bang your feet on the floor
tease (TEEZ) to make fun of somebody

Home and School Connection

Use this list of words from the book to help your child become a better reader. Word games and writing activities can help beginning readers reinforce literacy skills.

all	friends	nap	the
and	fun	need	their
anger	funny	not	they
angry	get	out	though
breath	gets	red	tired
brothers	glad	says	too
comes	gone	share	toys
dad	hot	snack	usually
deep	hug	sometimes	wait
don't	hungry	soon	when
everyone	inside	stamp	yell
face	mad	starts	
feels	make	take	
feet	mom	tease	

Index

About the Author

Tamra Orr has written more than 400 books for young people. The only thing she loves more than writing books is reading them. She lives in beautiful Portland, Oregon, with her husband, four children, dog, and cat. She only gets angry now and then.